FIRST BOOK OF GYPSY BALLADS

International English Edition

FIRST BOOK OF GYPSY BALLADS

FEDERICO GARCIA LORCA

FIRST BOOK OF GYPSY BALLADS: International English Edition

A Polyglot Press book.

Original title: **_Primer Romancero Gitano_** (1924-1927 by Federico García Lorca)

Translated by Jeffrey B Frazier

Art credit: Pen and ink drawings courtesy of Labiv. Labiv is a non-profit project of integrated interpretive art.

ISBN-13: 978-1-64809-002-8 (Omnilex Media)

Copyright © 2021 Jeffrey B Frazier

All rights reserved.

Contents

Preface   VII

Gyspsy Ballads

1. Ballad of the Moon   3
2. Precious and the Wind   5
3. Brawl   8
4. Sleepwalking Ballad   11
5. The Gyspy Nun   17
6. The Cheatin' Wife   19
7. Ballad of Despair   23
8. Saint Michael ~ Granada   27
9. Saint Raphael ~ Cordoba   31
10. Saint Gabriel ~ Seville   34
11. Arrest of Little Tony the Camborio
    on the Road to Seville   38
12. Death of Little Tony the Camborio   41
13. Dead from Love   45
14. Ballad of a Marked man   48
15. Ballad of the Spanish Civil Guard   51
16. The Martyrdom of Saint Eulalia   60
17. Mockery of Don Pedro on Horseback   64
18. Thamar and Amnon   70

Indexes   75

PREFACE

My desire is tinted green…

In his essay titled "*Shades of Green,*" prefacing another English translation of the *Romancero Gitano*, noted Lorca scholar Christopher Maurer documents no fewer than twenty unique English translations of Lorca's immortal opening line to the *Romance Sonámbulo*—"*Verde que te quiero verde.*" After carefully reviewing them all, and living for some time with the original, I chose a different path. In fact, I chose not one but two new English interpretations. I am pleased with the results. I hope you will be too.

During the translation process it was both a pleasure and a challenge to get to know the mind of Federico García Lorca through his own words at this early stage of his too-short career. In the process I made every effort I could think of to make sure that this work would be informed by his original genius and the environment that produced it.

It is true that literary translation is a risky act. Still, some works are so brilliant that they demand the attempt because they deserve the widest possible audience. It may also be true that every generation needs its own translation of major works—languages are living things that are always on the move, so we too must move if we want to keep up and remain relevant. Done well, I believe that a combination of the modern idiom linked with the past and all draped on the rhythmic framework inherent in a target language can be both faithful to the original art and pleasing to the senses.

In this translation I have used my best (and sometimes creative) judgment in the selection of vocabulary, meter, versification and rhyme that captures in English the essence of what Lorca's Spanish originals convey to me. In this new international edition, I have also incorporated a couple of genius touches inspired by another Lorca translator, Sarah Arvio, as seen in the titles to the poems *"The Cheatin' Wife,"* and *"Ballad of a Marked Man"*—I think her choices were spot on, and they are improvements on my original renderings.

In her fine work *Poet in Spain,* Arvio also notes that Lorca's original title for this collection of poems was "First Book of Gypsy Ballads" (*Primer Romancero Gitano*). Of course, the world was deprived of any possible companion volumes because of the brutality of prejudice and war. But though there may only ever be one volume, I have chosen to reflect the poet's original intention in the title to this edition. Taken as a whole, I hope this English rendering will sing a little and mesmerize and stick in the mind of English speakers the way Lorca's own words do in the Spanish-speaking world.

J. Frazier
02.14.2021

FIRST BOOK OF GYPSY BALLADS

#1

BALLAD OF THE MOON

To Conchita García Lorca

With her skirt of fragrant flowers
to the forge came the moon calling.
At her looks and looks the child.
The child is at her looking, looking.

The moon she parts her arms
and stirs the wind revealing
her alloyed breasts at once
profane and full of healing.

'Flee now moon, please fly away,
for if the gypsies come and find you
they'll steal your heart and turn it into
white necklaces and finger jewels.'

'Let me dance, my child,
and the gypsies on arrival,
your little eyes shut tightly
they'll find you on the anvil.'

'Flee now moon, please fly away,
I can hear their horses rumble.'
'Leave me child, just go just go,
my starchèd whiteness do not trample.'

Pounding the drum of the plain
closer came the riders.
Within the forge the child
has those eyes shut tighter.

Heads held high, eyes half shut,
through the olive grove they came—
bronzed gypsies all on horseback,
half asleep half in a dream.

How it sings up in the tree…
Listen to the night owl singing!
The moon she rises toward the sky,
to her hand a child is clinging.

Down in the forge they cry and cry,
the gypsies gnash and wail.
Now still, the wind keeps watch above.
Now watching, watching is the air.

#2

PRECIOUS AND THE WIND

To Dámaso Alonso

Playing on her parchment moon
along the way comes Precious,
accompanied by wreaths of laurel
her glassy path's amphibious.

The starless silence that is fleeing
from the pounding beat below
falls at the place where waves sing
of darkness where fish overflow.

The riflemen fall fast asleep
on the peaks of mountain ridges
as they guard the ivory towers
where the Englishmen do live.

And the gypsies of the water
raise for their amusement
fine monuments of snail shells
and boughs of pine so verdant.

Playing on her parchment moon
along the way comes Precious.
At her sight the wind whips up
for want of sleep turned vicious.

Unclothèd is Saint Christopher,
though cloakèd with his silver tongue,
as he spies the girl absorbed in
playing her sweet but careless song.

'Child, I've come to lift you up—
your dress that is, so I can see you.
Let my ancient fingers open
that blue rose inside your womb.'

Precious drops her tambourine
and runs and then runs faster.
But with his heated rapier
the brutish wind pursues her.

All the olive trees turn pale.
The sea's roar turns to frown.
Flutes ring out from shady spots,
as does from snow the slippery gong.

Run Precious! You had better run
before the green wind grabs you!

Run Precious! You had better run—
he is coming up behind you!
A satyr from the lower stars
with silver tongues of fire aglow.

Full of fear our Precious flees
and wanders through the pines.
She makes it to the house above,
an English diplomat she finds.

Startled by the howls and shouting
three riflemen come running fast
with caps surrounding all their temples
and tightly fitted cloaks of black.

The Englishman gives to the gypsy
warm milk as well as a stiff shot.
Our Precious takes the glass of milk,
declines the gin and starts to sob.

Now safe inside the girl recounts
through sobs and sighs her tale of woe,
while up above on tiles of slate
the biting wind deals furious blows.

#3

BRAWL

To Rafael Méndez

Covered with the blood of rivals,
halfway down the steep ravine,
the shiny knives of Albacete
like silver fish in sunlight gleam.

Silhouetted in a bitter green,
and the harsh light of their fate,
we see the outlines of the riders
and their horses all irate.

In the arms of an olive tree
two old women sit there weeping
while the brawling bull in question
charges up over the railing.

Hankerchiefs and cool snow-water
brought black angels to the site.
Angels with great wings resembling
Albacete's shiny knives.

Juan Antonio from Montilla
dead on the slope is rolling down,
his body filled with lilies while
pomegranate stains his brow.
A cross of fire his death wagon,
now he rides a different mount.

The judge, along with Civil Guards,
approaches through the olive grove.
As a serpent's silent song
one can hear the blood-slick moan.

'Officers it seems we have here
just a minor umbrage—
four Romans dead upon the ground
and also five from Carthage.'

At these words and heated rumors
the afternoon, mad as a hatter,
faints and falls into the laps
of all the wounded horseback riders.

Then black angels fly away
on the west wind as it roils.

Angels with their braided tresses.
Angels with their hearts of oil.

#4

SLEEPWALKING BALLAD

To Gloria Giner and Fernando de los Ríos

My desire is tinted green.
Green the branches. Green the wind.
The ship upon the sea below
the horse up in the hills.

Shadows falling on her waist,
on her balcony she dreams.
Flesh of green, now green her hair,
her frozen eyes a silver stream.

Oh green, how I would have you green.
Under the gypsy moon,
the things below that at her gaze
are far removed from her dim view.

✼

Oh green, how I would have you green.
Huge stars approach from far beyond,

looming dark and frozen
they point the way towards dawn.

With its abrasive branches
the fig tree scrubs the wind.
And like a wildcat's claws
the tall grass stands and stiffens.

But who shall come? And whence?
On her balcony she stays,
flesh of green and green her hair.
A sea of bitterness holds sway.

'Brother, let me trade
my horse for your abode,
my saddle for your mirror,
my blade for your bedclothes.
Brother, I come bleeding
from Cabra's passes down below.'

'My boy, I'd gladly make that trade
if that were in my power.
But I am not myself you see, and
this is now my home no longer.'

'Brother, let me die
a decent death at home.

On a bed of steel perhaps,
with silken sheets from Rome.
Surely you can see my wound
slit from my breast to throat?'

'I see your oozing bloody sash
stained with those death markers.
Three hundred drying roses
your fine white shirt make darker.
But I am not myself you see, and
this is now my home no longer.'

'Then let me climb at least
up to the rails of green
to the balconies up high.
Oh let me, let me please!
To the railings of the moon
from where the water screams.'

So towards the balconies up high
the two companions' climb begins.
Trailing tears behind them
a trace of blood marks where they've been.
On the roof were trembling
little lanterns of cheap tin.
A thousand glassy tambourines
wounded dawn with their loud din.

✣

Oh green, how I would have you green.
Green the branches. Green the wind.
Up they went, and up some more,
the two companions rose again.
In their mouths strange tastes of gall,
and mint, and basil and the wind.

'Where is she brother? Tell me!
Where is your girl so bitter?
How long she waited for you!
How long she sought your glimmer,
her face made up, her hair still black,
on this green balcony it shimmered.'

✣

Above the well the gypsy sways
from side to side it seems.
Flesh of green, now green her hair,
her frozen eyes a silver stream.
Above the water she's aloft
held by an icicle of moonbeam.

Then like in tiny courtyards
the night turned still and cozy,
though drunken officers below
pounded and demanded entry.

Oh green, how I would have you green.
Green the branches. Green the wind.
The ship upon the sea below
the horse up in the hills.

FIRST BOOK OF GYPSY BALLADS ~ FEDERICO GARCÍA LORCA

"Hungry for More"

#5

THE GYPSY NUN

To José Moreno Villa

Silence of quicklime and myrtle.
Wild mallow in fine herbs.
God's bride embroiders giliflowers
upon sackcloth deserved.

Seven flying rainbow birds
grace a grayed-out chandelier.
Like a bear lying belly-up
the church she growls, but she's not near.

How well she stitches! With such grace!
Upon the sackcloth she embroiders
flowers of her fantasies—
some with saffron, some magnolias.

What a sunflower! What moons!
Those spangled ribbons are not crass.
It's not a tablecloth for tea,
it's altar cloth for holy mass.

In the nearby kitchen
five grapefruit halves are soaking.

They're like the Christ's five wounds of lore
in Almería cut and candied.

Two horsemen gallop by the nun,
at least that's what she thinks…
Their final muffled rumor looses
the buttons on her silk chemise.

While she gazes at the sky
and the mountains in the distance
of sugar and lemon verbena
her sweet heart it breaks again.

How steep the walk across the plain
with twenty suns ablaze on high!
And just to glimpse her fantasy
how rivers rise and flow upright!

In the breeze play the sun's rays
their game of chess above her window
while she continues to embroider
all her herbs and flowers below.

#6

THE CHEATIN' WIFE

To Lydia Cabrera and her negrita

I took her to the riverside
thinking she was single,
but she was another's bride.

It happened all on St. Jame's eve.
I felt almost as if compelled,
as the light from street lamps faded
and the crickets cast their spell.

I dared to touch the edges
of her breasts as they were sleeping,
then like hyacinth bouquets
they all at once were on me blooming.

The starch of her white petticoats
sounded in my ears
like a piece of silken cloth
slit by a dozen spears.

With no silver light to crown them
trees upon the banks grew bigger.

And many hounds on the horizon
howled from far beyond the river.

※

Beyond the brambles, reeds and thorns
a spot for us I found,
beside the river's underbrush
upon the silty ground.

I removed my tie.
She took off her dress.
Me, my gun and holster;
she, her slips and bodice.

Neither shells nor lilies
glow with skin so fine,
nor prisms splitting moonlight
with such splendor shine.

Her thighs slipped from my gentle grasp,
half frozen half on fire,
like a school of silver fish
startled with desire.

That night I rode like I have never
down a road by bliss surrounded
with no stirrup, with no bridle,
upon a pearly filly mounted.

Discretion and my chivalry
demand that I do not reveal
the bright illumination from
the things she whispered in my ear.

Covered both with sand and kisses
I led her from the river pleased
as the lily swords behind us
waged a battle with the breeze.

I rushed in like a true bull—
like a gypsy should.
I gave to her a sewing box
of satin and of wood.

But I couldn't fall in love
because she was another's bride.
She told me was single when
I took her to the riverside.

First Book of Gypsy Ballads ~ Federico García Lorca

"Human sexuality"

BALLAD OF DESPAIR

To José Navarro Pardo

The roosters picks are picking
when seeking dawn's first flush
along comes Soledad Montoya
through the darkened brush.

With an air of horse and shadow
and her flesh of yellowed bronze
her breasts are smoky anvils
groaning out their rounded songs.

'Soledad, why do you call
at this late hour and all alone?'
'What does it matter to you then
who I seek or what I moan?
I come in search of my true self,
my happiness and sense of home.'

'Soledad of all my sorrows
don't you know that any steed
run riot loses all control
and ends up swallowed by the sea?'

'Don't speak to me of ocean waves.
The true source of despair
springs from the land of olive groves
and leaves that rustle in the air.'

'Soledad so full of sorrow,
what pity and what pain!
You weep the juice of bitter lemons—
the taste of all your wait in vain.'

'The weight is more than I can bear!
I pace my house from room to room.
I drag my two black braids behind—
a kitchen and a bedroom broom.

The weight is turning to jet black
my flesh and all my closet.
Oh my blouses of fine linen!
Oh my thighs of poppy flowers!'

'In the water of the larks
wash your body, my poor Lonely,
It will leave your heart at peace
my dear Soledad Montoya.'

✼

From below the river sings:
ruffled sky and frilly leaves.

With scores of pumpkin flowers now
the new light up above is wreathed.

Oh the burden of the gypsies!
A pain so clean and all alone.
The pain of hidden rivers
and a dawn so damn remote.

First Book of Gypsy Ballads ~ Federico García Lorca

"Things to know which cannot be known"

#8

SAINT MICHAEL ~ GRANADA

To Diego Buigas de Dalmau

Loaded down with sunflowers
I see mules upon the trails
of the mountain, mountain, mountain.
I see their shadows from the rails.

In shady spots their eyes grow dull,
by night's dim vastness tarnished.
In the twists and bends of air
starts to rustle dawn all brackish.

A heaven of white mules below
closes its quick-silver eyes
lending to the semi-darkness
a final air of heart's desire.

When the water goes all frigid
no one dares to touch that fountain.
Frenzied water in the open
from the mountain, mountain,
mountain.

✼

Saint Michael the archangel now
from his towering bed on high,
garlanded by lace and lanterns,
shows off his propitious thighs.

Tamed by the ringing of the bell
our angel at the strike of twelve
feigns a sweet perturbance with
the feathers of the nightengales.

Saint Michael sings upon the panes;
three thousand nights of youth,
perfumed by herbs and oils yet
far from the wildflowers, in truth.

✼

Down on the beach the sea he dances
a poem of balconies on high.
And the edges of the moon
lose their reeds while voices rise.

Along come luscious ladies now
eating seeds of sunflowers,
concealing huge behinds that loom
like spatial orbs of burnished copper.

And gentlemen of standing
with ladies wearing veils
of sadness and nostalgia for
lost songs of youthful nightengales.
In the church Manila's bishop,
poor and blinded by the saffron,
a double-sided mass pronounces—
one for men and one for women.

In the bedroom of his tower
Saint Michael bides his time enjoying
the spangles and the sequins that
adorn his lacy underclothing.

Saint Michael holds his court above,
of balloons and all odd numbers king,
while from the finest berberesque
glass balconies comes cheering.

"City at the sea in one thousand years
of perfect peace"

#9

SAINT RAPHAEL ~ CORDOBA

To Juan Izquierdo Croselles

I

Among the reeds along the shore
covered carriages they used to
arrive upon the river banks where
waves would polish Roman statues.

'Twixt thunderclouds and flower beds
reflected on those waters glassy
all those carriages knew well
Guadalquivir's great river valley.

The children sing and weave a tale
of a world that's now disheartened,
close by old covered carriages
float lost upon the waters darkened.

But Cordoba she does not tremble
beneath the strange confusion
for when the misty architecture
dissipates its smoky fumes

a chaste and glowing visage of
her bony marble base resumes.
Upon the arches of her triumph
unfurl thin petals made of tin
embroidering pure shades of gray,
rustling as if from the wind.

And as the bridge whispers and blows
ten murmurs of god Neptune
tobacco sellers down below
flee along the walls in ruin.

II

A single fish within the water
of two Cordobas makes juncture:
plain Cordoba among the reeds; and,
Cordoba of architecture.

Children with impassive faces
on the riverbanks undress.
Merlins at the waist they are and
to Tobias all apprenticed.

So they can tease that single fish
with questions all ironic, like:
Do you want some wine flowers now,
or perhaps some cartwheel dives?

But the fish who gilds the water,
if the marble works he darkens,
teaches them a balanced lesson
like a solitary column.
Then the Archangel all adorned
by sequins darker than a cave
seeks gossip and a cradle in
the churning discourse of the waves.

A single fish within the water.
Two Cordobas, both beautiful—
Cordoba split by streams below;
gaunt Cordoba celestial.

#10

SAINT GABRIEL ~ SEVILLE

To don Agustín Viñuales

I

A handsome reed of a fine youth
broad of shoulder, slender figure,
with skin like midnight's apple and
his sinews hot like silver,
wanders 'round a street deserted—
small sad mouth but eyes much bigger.

His patent leather shoes are singing,
trampling dahlias on the breeze,
in their bifurcated rhythms
dirges brief and heavenly.

Along the banks there are not any
palms to rival his smooth groove—
no emperor with golden crown,
no starry mount that's on the move.

When he tilts his head so slightly
down toward his jasper chest
nighttime seeks a plain of worship
wanting to kneel down and rest.

Saint Gabriel the Archangel,
the fancier of moth and pigeon,
and scourge of all the willow trees—
all lonely guitars play for him.

'Saint Gabriel: the child is crying
in his mother's womb.
Don't you forget now that the gypsies
clothed you from the weaver's loom.'

II

Poorly dressed, lit by the moon,
Annunciation of the Kings
now opens up the entry gate
for the steed that is approaching.

Saint Gabriel the Archangel,
great-grandson of the bell tower,
half lily and half smile
comes a-calling ever closer.

Within his fine embroidered vest
hidden crickets chirp in time.

Those stars from up above at night
turn into little tinkling chimes.

'Oh Gabriel, canst thou see me here
piercèd thrice with happiness?
Thy brightness opens jasmine flowers
upon my visage luminous.'

'May God keep thee our dear Lady,
dark-skinned beauty of our wonder.
Thou shalt bear a child divine
more beautiful than wind and clover.'

'Oh my little Gabriel!
Saint Gabriel of creation!
I wouldst have thee sit upon
a throne made from carnations.'

'May God keep thee our dear Lady,
poorly dressed, lit by the moon.
Thy child shall have upon his chest
one mole and three dark bloody wounds.'

'Oh Gabriel, how thou dost shine!
Saint Gabriel of my dreams!
Deep down inside my virgin breasts
is born a milky stream.'

'May God keep thee our dear Lady,
mother to the dynasties.
Although thine eyes may still be dry
from landscapes crossed by donkeys.'

The child sings upon the breast
of our dear Lady who is surprised—
three slugs of raw green almond there
do tremble in his little cry.

But Gabriel upon the air
a saintly staircase he is climbing.
And the nighttime stars above
have turned to flowers everlasting.

#11

ARREST OF LITTLE TONY THE CAMBORIO ON THE ROAD TO SEVILLE

To Margarita Xirgu

Antonio Torres Heredia,
from Camborios descended,
heads to Seville to see the bulls
a willow switch in his hand bended.

Swarthy like an olive moon
he takes a slow and jaunty pace.
His oily ringlets dangle down
glistening upon his face.

Half way to his destination
he cuts citrus from the trees
and tosses it into the water
gilding it with lemon spheres.

And half way to his destination
the Civil Guards there on patrol
from under branches of an elm tree
bind him, lead him off in tow.

Like a cape upon a shoulder
slowly slips away the day,
lengthening as it descends
down the streams into the bay.

Awaiting Capricorn above
all the olive groves are still,
while a gentle equine breeze
leaps across the leaden hills.

Antonio Torres Heredia,
from Camborios descended,
now comes without his willow switch
by those five Civil Guards commended.

'Who are you really, Anthony?
Were you a true Camborio
you would have made a fountain of
our blood in five streams pouring.
You are the son of no one,
much less a true Camborio.'

All the gypsies now are gone
who dared to cross alone the mounts!
All their dusty daggers now
shiver underneath the ground.

At the stroke of nine they take him
off to jail to face his fate
while the Civil Guard patrol
passes 'round the lemonade.

And also at the stroke of nine
they close the jail with a loud thump,
all while the sky above is gleaming
like a colt's luminous rump.

#12

DEATH OF LITTLE TONY THE CAMBORIO

To José Antonio Rubio Sacristán

Near the river Guadalquivir
rumors of his death were heard.
A virile voice of sweet carnation
by ancient rumors was interred.

Like a biting wild boar
he set upon their cowboy boots.
In the slippery struggle he leapt
like a dolphin breaking loose.

His tie turned crimson with their blood
fending off four dagger blows, but
those four blows were four too many—
he by force gave up the ghost.

When the stars all stab and pound
their iron spikes into gray water,
when the bull calves' dreams are full of
flapping capes of wistful wallflowers,

rumors of his death are heard near
Guadalquivir the ancient river.

'Antonio Torres Heredia,
Camborio all hardened,
swarthy like an olive moon
a virile voice of sweet carnation:
down by the river Guadalquivir
who has your life just cruelly taken?'

'My four cousins, all Heredias,
beloved sons of Benamejí.
What they did not mind on others
they coveted when found on me.

My fine shoes with hues of currant,
my ivory medallions,
my face's fine complexion of
green olive and of jasmine.'

'Oh little Tony the Camborio,
like an Empress dignified!
Say your prayers and cross yourself
because you are about to die.'

'Oh, Federico call the guards!
Tell them to come hence and quickly!

My body like a rod has snapped,
oh Federico García!'

Bleeding out upon his side,
three bloody bursts laid him down low.
I wager we shall never see
a repetition of that show.

A lively angel placed his head
upon a cushion lightly.
Others of a tired mien
the oil lamps lit brightly.

And when the cousins make it home,
beloved sons of Benamejí,
death's rumors were extinguished by
the river called Guadalquivir.

First Book of Gypsy Ballads ~ Federico García Lorca

"What drugs can do to you"

#13

DEAD FROM LOVE

To Margarita Manso

'Through those passageways up high
what do I spy that gleams unhidden?'

   'Close the door my precious child:
   the clock has just now struck eleven.'

'In my gaze I spy four lampposts
shining in my eyes unbidden.'

   'It must be the people come to
   polish copper in the kitchen.'

Draped in fancy yellow tresses
are the rigid yellow towers,
all thanks to the waning moon—
a garlic clove of shrinking silver.

On the windows of the ledges
night comes calling with a tremor,

a thousand dogs in hot pursuit
and yet they still don't recognize her.
And from those passageways on high
down wafts a scent of wine and amber.

�

Through the arch laid waste by midnight
echoes of old voices sound
and breezes of sweet sugarcane
float across the dampened ground.

The oxen and the roses slept
yet in those corridors up high
with the furor of Saint George were
clamoring those four bright lights.

Sad women of the valley floor
let their blood of man subside.
Blood quiet as cut flowers and
blood as bitter as young thighs.

Old women from the river cried
at the bottom of the mountain
stuck in an unending loop of
flowing hair and reputation.

Whitewashed walls lent to the night
their squareness and their whiteness

while seraphim and gypsies played
soft songs upon their concertinas.

'Mother, when my time has come
and I'm about to die
send out to all the gentlemen
blue telegrams both far and wide.'

Then in the darkened halls below
seven cries and seven wounds.
Seven double poppies bleeding,
breaking melancholy moons.

Full of wounded hands
and little crowns of flowers
an ocean of profanity
was heard from out of nowhere.

On those echoes from the forest
heaven slammed its heavy door
while in the corridors up high
the lights kept up their shiny clamor.

#14

BALLAD OF A MARKED MAN

For Emilio Aladrén

My lonliness it never ends!

Little eyes upon my body
and the large ones on my horse,
never close when night falls
nor do they deviate from north
where a dream of thirteen ships
slips softly from us on its course.

Instead my eyes continue north,
shield bearers in a wakeful state.
They're clean and hard and fixed upon
those metals and those cliffs of slate—
there consulting frozen cards
lies my body stripped of veins.

There ponderous water buffalo
toward the little boys are charging

as they bathe themsleves in moons
of their graceful horns all wavy.

And upon sleepwalking anvils
all the hammers they were ringing
the sleeplessness of horse and rider.
Song of insomnia they were singing.

✤

On the twenty-fifth of June
came the message to Amargo:
'If you like you now can cut
the oleanders on your patio.

Upon your door please paint a cross
and sign your name beside it,
for hemlock plants and nettles
shall take root in your side,
and biting at your shoes will be
moist needles of quicklime.

It will be at nighttime in
the tall magnetic mountains
where water buffalo do drink
in dreaming reeds as from a fountain.

Learn to fold your arms, sir.
Order lights and bells, don't wait.

Taste the coldness of the breeze,
of metals and those cliffs of slate.
For in two months your shroud arrives
and you shall lie in wake.'

✤

Through the misty air Saint James
swings his hazy broadsword.
From the warpèd sky behind
a solemn silence softly flows.

✤

Amargo opened up his eyes
on the twenty-fifth of June.
On August twenty-fifth he then
laid down to close them far too soon.

To see the shadow of the doomed
people came from far and wide.
The restful shadow on the wall
his endless lonliness belied.

And how impeccable his shroud,
creased smartly like a Roman valance.
The straightness of those linen folds
gave to his death a certain balance.

#15

BALLAD OF THE SPANISH CIVIL GUARD

To Juan Guerrero
Consul General of Poetry

Blackened are their horses.
Their iron shoes are black.
Upon their capes are shining
ink stains and bits of wax.

You'll never see them crying
for their skulls are full of lead.
With souls of patent leather you can
hear them on the highway tread.

Hunchbacked creatures of the night,
wherever they go they command
the silences of darkened rubber
and the fears of sifting sand.

They go wherever they may please,
in their heads some vague abstraction,
some imprecise astronomy
hidden in their dreams of handguns.

✽

Oh city of the gypsies!
Flags on your corners and your curves.
The harvest moon and pumpkin form
a vital part of your preserves.

Oh city of the gypsies!
Once seen she cannot be forgotten.
City of pain and grief and musk
with towers of fine cinnamon.

✽

When the night was on approach,
and what a nightly night arose,
the gypsies were down in their forges
shaping suns and iron arrows.

A horse that had been wounded
went slowly calling door to door.
Glass roosters with their rooster songs
near Jerez de la Frontera crowed.

The swirling wind had soon denuded
the corner of surprise
on that silvery nightly night—
oh what a nightly night did rise.

�֎

Saint Joseph and his Virgin bride
have lost their little castanets
and so come looking for the gypsies
who might disgorge them with regrets.

The Virgin comes dressed to the nines
in foil paper bright like diamonds,
like a mayoress bedecked with
a necklace of Marcona almonds.

Beneath his silken cape
Saint Joseph moves his arms.
Behind him proceeds Pedro Domecq
in company of three Persian sultans.

Up high, about an ecstasy of storks,
the partial moon is dreaming.
By banners rooftops are invaded
and by lanterns softly gleaming.

Dancing girls bereft of hips
in the mirrors there are sobbing.
Water and shadow, shadow and water
near Jerez de la Frontera flowing.

Oh city of the gypsies!
Flags on your corners and your curves.
Extinguish your green lanterns now
for coming are those sworn to serve.

Oh city of the gypsies!
Once seen she cannot be forgotten.
Without a comb for her long braids,
far from the sea leave her besotted.

�֎

Towards the city all adorned
two by two they are advancing.
Encroaching on their holsters is
the din of flowers everlasting.

Two by two they are advancing
this twin nocturne clothed as such.
To them a showcase for their spurs
the sky above is just so much.

✦

The city, feeling free from fear,
had multiplied its doorfronts.
But forty civil guards are now
bursting through them like a stormfront.

Time stood still on all the clocks,
while trying to avoid suspicion
all the brandy in the bottles
like November they disguised them.

In the weathervanes above
arose a flight of screams.
Trampled by the hooves below
sabres sliced the sullen breeze.

Along the darkened streets in town
old gypsy women run and flee
with their jars of silver coins
and the horses fast asleep.

Coming up the steepest streets
are cloaks all black and sinister
leaving in their fleeting wake
tiny little whirlwind scissors.

The gypsies now are gathering
by the gates of Bethlehem.
Saint Joseph (he himself now wounded)
shrouds in white a fallen maiden.

Repeating all throughout the night
are rifles sharp and stubborn.
With the spittle of the stars
the Virgin Mary soothes the children.

But the Civil Guards advance
sowing seeds of bonfires
where youthful imagination burns
denuded by desires.

Moaning is Rosa of the Camborios
seated in her doorway
with both her newly severed breasts
all heaped upon a silver tray.
By their braids pursued
many other maidens run,
with roses of black powder
bursting bursting all around them.

Then when all the roofs above
turned furrows down below
the dawn she shrugged her shoulders
in a long profile of stone.

Oh, city of the gypsies!
The Civil Guard is leaving
through a silent tunnel
with flickering flames encroaching.

Oh, city of the gypsies!
Once seen, by all you are remembered

in a game of hide and seek—
moon and sand paired on my forehead.

THREE HISTORICAL BALLADS

First Book of Gypsy Ballads ~ Federico García Lorca

"Judgement Day"

#16

THE MARTYRDOM OF SAINT EULALIA

To Rafael Martinez Nadal

I
PANORAMA OF MERIDA

Through the streets do run and prance
horses with long tails and manes
while aging Roman soldiers gamble
or nod off after their card games.

Half a mountain of Minervas
spreads its leafless arms aloft
while water in suspension forms
gilding ridges of the rocks.

The night of stars with broken noses
and of torsos lying prone
waits to bring it tumbling down
at the early crack of dawn.

Blasphemies red-crested
from time to time ring out.

With her shrieks the holy girl
shatters all the crystal goblets.

Knives are honed upon a wheel
and sharpened hooks are forged.
Merida she is thus crowned,
as the bull of the anvil roars,
with stalks of wild berries
and waking fragrant flora.

II
THE MARTYRDOM

Flora now denuded climbs
up a little water staircase.
To carry Eulalia's severed breasts
the consul seeks a silver tray.

A gushing stream from greenish veins
from her throat now gurgles.
Her feminity is trembling
like a bird caught in the brambles.

Aimlessly along the ground
her severed hands are creeping—
still capable in headless prayer,
sign of the cross they make while leaping.

Through the bloody gaping holes
that once her breasts maintained
tiny heavens are beheld
and milk in whitish strains.
Blanketing her back side
a thousand bloody little trees.
The incisions of the flames
with their moisture they impede.

Sleepless yellow centurions,
with their grayed-out skin,
their silver armor chiming,
arrive in heaven with their din.

While in confusèd passion
the manes and swords still vibrate
the smoky breasts of Saint Eulalia
the consul carries on a tray.

III
HELL AND GLORY

Undulating snow reposes.
Eulalia dangles from a tree.
The charcoal of her nakedness
smudges breezes cold and icy.

The night shines with a certain taughtness.
Dead Eulalia in the tree.
The inkwells of the cities
spill their ink but very slowly.

Covering the snowy fields
are rows of tailors' mannequins.
They bemoan in long black lines
their mutilated silences.

Then a partial snow commences.
White Eulalia in the tree.
Piercing shiny nickel squares
fill her side with carpentry.

Shining over burned out skies
among the gurgling streams
and nightengales on boughs of pine
a shiny golden monstrance gleams.
White Eulalia in the whiteness.
Colored glass begins to leap!
Seraphim and angels chanting:

HOLY! HOLY! HOLY!

#17

MOCKERY OF DON PEDRO ON HORSEBACK

BALLAD WITH LAGOONS—WATERY GAPS

To Jean Cassau

Don Pedro weeping
pulls astride.
A gentle rider,
how he cries!

Mounted on a bitless steed,
in its gait a certain grace,
he comes in search of daily bread
and of kisses on the face.

To the wind above
all the windows inquire
about the dark lament
of the gentle rider.

FIRST LAGOON

Under the water

the words continue.
Over the water
a rounded moon
bathes herself
causing envy in the other.
How high!

On the banks
a child
sees the moons and says:
'Play your cymbals!' to the night

CONTINUE

To a far off city
Don Pedro has arrived.
Among a forest of cedars
the city of gold it shines.
Bethlehem perhaps? Rosemary and
verbena are alight.

The terraces are shining
along with clouds up high,
while under fallen arches
the gentle rider rides.

An old man and two women
emerge to greet Don Pedro,

bearing silver oil lamps
they meet him at the door.

The poplars saying 'no' are heard.
The nightingale says 'we shall see.'

SECOND LAGOON

Under the water
the words continue.
Over the water's wavy hair
a circle of birds and flames.
And through the fields of sugarcane,
witnesses who know what's missing.
Aimless strains from a guitar
form a concrete dream.

CONTINUE

The old man and two women
bearing silver oil lamps
head toward the cemetery
along the flat part of the path.

Among the flowers of saffron,
in a somber breeze,
the lamp bearers encounter
Don Pedro's fallen steed.

Bleating through the skies was heard
a secret voice of dusk forlorn.
While a unicorn of absence
on crystal glass breaks its sole horn.

The great and far off city
now in flames is burning,
while a man turns inland
accompanied by tears and sobbing.

To the North there is one star.
To the South a sailor.

FINAL LAGOON

Under the water
are the words.
A slush of voices foresaken.
On chilly lily pads above
lies Don Pedro all forgotten—

Oh! With the frogs he's playing.

FIRST BOOK OF GYPSY BALLADS ~ FEDERICO GARCÍA LORCA

"Time experiment including past and future"

First Book of Gypsy Ballads ~ Federico García Lorca

"The fight between good and evil"

#18

THAMAR AND AMNON

For Alfonso García-Valdecasas

The moon revolves up in the sky
over a parchèd landscape
while the summer she is sowing
hints of tiger and of flame.

Above all of the rooftops
metallic nerves were ringing out.
With approaching wooly bleats
rings of air made bleating sounds.

Full of healed-up wounds
the earth offers herself up,
or shudders from the cauteries of
white lights razor sharp.

Of birdsong in her muted throat
Thamar she was a-dreaming
to the sound of moonlit citars
and frigid frozen tambourines.

Her nakedness in the dark eaves,
like a palm's sharp north,
seeks snowflakes from her womb
and from her back hailstones.

Naked on the terrace
Thamar she was a-singing.
Surrounding her two little feet
five pigeons there were freezing.

Amnon, solid and quite thin,
at the tower was a-gazing
his loins all full of fuming foam
while his beard was oscillating.

Stretched out on the terrace
her nakedness was shining brightly.
She was like a piercing arrow,
his teeth therefore were clenching tightly.

On the low and rounded moon
Amnon's eyes were fixed and gazing
spying by the moonlight there
the firm breasts of his naked sibling.

Stretched out on his bed
was Amnon at three-thirty,

his whole bedroom suffering
from his eyes so full of wings.

Whole villages in brown sand
the solid light she buries
or finds in some transition there
rose coral and bright dahlias.

The lymph of an oppressèd well
into clay jars its silence leaks.
Midst the moss of tree trunks
the stretched out cobra sings.

For the coolness of his bed
Amnon now is moaning.
His burning flesh is covered by
a shivering green ivy.

To his quiet alcove now
Thamar approaches softly,
her veins are as the Danube—
wavy, blue and cloudy.

'Blind my eyes dear sister
with your dawn so firm.
My threads of blood are weaving
those ruffles on your skirt.'

'Brother, leave me be.
Your kisses, breezy and warm,
are just like wasps upon my back—
like tiny flutes in double swarm.'

'Thamar, two fishes call me
from your breasts so high
and upon your fingertips
pent-up roses sigh.'

Neighing in the courtyard were
one hundred horses of the king,
while the grapevines young and slender
pails of sunlight were enduring.

Now he takes her by the hair.
Now he rips off her chemise.
Corals on a blonde map sketch out
tiny lukewarm flowing streams.

Over all the houses
screams were heard like thunder.
What a thicket of knives
and tunics torn asunder!

Up and down sad stairwells slaves
keep a-coming and a-going.
Under the still clouds above
pistons and young thighs are pounding.

All around Thamar
are gypsy virgins screaming.
Drops from her now martyred flower
other virgins are collecting.

In the closed off chambers
all the sheets turn red from white.
While the fishes and the grape leaves
the hoped-for desperate dawn belie.

Amnon flees upon his horse,
a furious violator.
Black men aim their arrows at him
from the walls and watchtowers.

And when his steed's four hooves
become a distant murmur
King David with a steady hand
his harp strings severs with a scissor.

INDEXES

Index of Poem Titles

Arrest of Little Tony the Camborio on the Road to Seville 38
Ballad of Despair 23
Ballad of a Marked Man 48
Ballad of the Moon 3
Ballad of the Spanish Civil Guard 51
Brawl 8
Dead from Love 45
Death of Little Tony the Camborio 41
Martyrdom of Saint Eulalia 60
Mockery of Don Pedro on Horseback 64
Precious and the Wind 5
Saint Gabriel (Sevilla) 34
Saint Michael (Granada) 27
Saint Raphael (Córdoba) 31
Sleepwalking Ballad 11
Thamar and Amnon 70
The Gypsy Nun 17
The Cheatin' Wife 19

Index of First Lines

A handsome reed of a fine youth 34
Among the reeds along the shore 31
Antonio Torres Heredia 38
Blackened are their horses 51
Covered with the blood of rivals 8
Don Pedro weeping 64
I took her to the riverside 19
Loaded down with sunflowers. 27
My desire is tinted green 11
My lonliness it never ends! 48
Near the river Guadalquivir 41
Playing on her parchment moon 5
Silence of quicklime and myrtle 17
The moon revolves up in the sky 70
The roosters picks are picking 23
Through the streets do run and prance 60
Through those passageways up high 45
With her skirt of fragrant flowers 3

Index of Symbols, Key Words and Images

air 27, 37
    a somber breeze..............66
    leaves that rustle in the air......................24
    the breeze ..18, 21, 34, 50, 55
    the misty air......................50
angels
    A lively angel.....................43
    angel.......................28
    archangel............................28
    Archangel...................33, 35
    black angels.....................8, 9
balconies................... 13, 28, 29
    green balcony...................14
    on her balcony she dreams..........................11
blood... 8, 9, 13, 39, 41, 46, 72
    Bleeding out upon his side..................43
    blood of man.....................46
    bloody sash........................13
    greenish veins..................61
    I come bleeding...............12
    pomegranate stains his brow................... 9
    seven double poppies bleeding........................47
    three bloody bursts.......43
    three dark bloody wounds..........................36
    Three hundred drying roses..............................13
blue..6, 72
    blue telegrams.................47

breasts..... 3, 19, 36, 56, 62, 71, 73
    her breasts are smoky anvils..............................23
    severed breasts...............61
    sings upon the breast...37
children
    child....3, 4, 35, 36, 37, 45, 65
    Child......................... 6
civil authorities
    Civil Guard................ 40, 56
    Civil Guard patrol..........40
    Civil Guards...9, 38, 39, 56
    drunken officers.............14
    forty civil guards............54
    judge......................... 9
    Officers................................ 9
    the guards.........................42
    three riflemen................... 7
death..9, 12, 13, 41, 42, 43, 50
    cemetery.............................66
    you shall lie in wake......50
    your shroud.......................50
dream.............................. 4, 48, 66
fauna
    a bear lying belly-up.....17
    a colt's luminous rump 40
    a thousand dogs..............46
    a wildcat's claws.............12
    brawling bull...................... 8
    bull calves.........................41
    bulls......................................38
    cobra....................................72
    Corals..................................73

crickets 19, 35
dolphin 41
donkeys 37
fish 5, 8, 20, 32, 33
fishes 73, 74
frogs 67
heaven of white mules . 27
larks 24
many dogs 20
mules upon the trails 27
night owl 4
nightengales 28, 29, 63
nightingale 66
oxen 46
pigeons 71
rainbow birds 17
roosters 23, 52
serpent 9
snail shells 5
tiger 70
wasps 73
water buffalo 48, 49
wild boar 41
fire 7, 9
   half on fire 20
   the flames encircling 56
flora
   almonds 53
   bitter lemons 24
   boughs of pine 5, 63
   brambles, reeds and
      thorns 20
   carnations 36
   citrus 38
   dahlias 34, 72
   elm tree 38
   fig tree 12
   five grapefruit halves 17
   forest 47, 65
   giliflowers 17

grapevines 73
half lily and half smile .. 35
hemlock 49
hyacinth bouquets 19
jasmine 36, 42
laurel 5
lemon verbena 18
lilies 9, 20
lily pads 67
lily swords 21
Minervas 60
moss of tree trunks 72
myrtle 17
oleanders 49
palms 34
pines 7
poplars 66
poppy flowers 24
pumpkin 25, 52
pumpkin flowers 25
raw green almond 37
rose 6
rose coral 72
roses 46, 73
seeds of sunflowers 28
sugarcane 66
sunflower 17
sweet carnation 41, 42
sweet sugarcane 46
tall grass 12
trees upon the banks 19
verbena 65
wild berries 61
Wild mallow 17
wildflowers 28
wistful wallflowers 41
flowers 3, 17, 18, 32, 36, 37,
   54, 61, 66
   crowns of flowers 47
   cut flowers 46

martyred flower..............74
forge............................3, 4
   anvil 3, 61
   forges....................52
   hammers they were
      ringing............................49
   sleepwalking anvils.......49
gods
   May God keep thee 36, 37
   Neptune..............................32
green 6, 11, 12, 13, 14, 15
   bitter green.......................... 8
   green ivy 72
   green lanterns...................54
   Green the branches 11,
      14, 15
   Green the wind 11, 15
   verdant................................. 5
gypsies.. 3, 4, 5, 25, 35, 39, 47,
   52, 53, 54, 56, 57
   Gypsies 55
   gypsy 7, 11, 14, 21
   GYPSY NUN.......................17
   gypsy virgins.....................74
   old gypsy women............55
hair
   braided tresses................10
   By their braids pursued
     56
   flowing hair.......................46
   green her hair... 11, 12, 14
   her hair still black 14
   long braids..........................54
   oily ringlets 38
   two black braids..............24
herbs and spices
   basil...14
   cinnamon............................52
   fine herbs 17
   herbs............................. 18, 28

   mint..14
   Rosemary 65
   saffron.................. 17, 29, 66
   tobacco 32
horse..... 11, 12, 15, 23, 48, 49,
   52, 74
horses.......... 4, 8, 51, 55, 60, 73
   a bitless steed...................64
   a different mount.............. 9
   a gentle equine breeze.39
   a pearly filly 20
   any steed.............................23
   fallen steed 66
   gentle rider............... 64, 65
   horsemen 18
   my saddle...........................12
   riders............................4, 8, 9
   starry mount.....................34
   steed 74
   their spurs..........................54
   Trampled by the hooves
      below 55
moon 3, 4, 5, 6, 13, 28, 35, 36,
   53, 65, 70, 71
   gypsy moon.......................11
   harvest moon 52
   icicle of moonbeam 14
   moonlight.................. 20, 71
   moons 17, 47, 49, 65
   olive moon 38
   the waning moon............45
musical instruments
   A thousand glassy
      tambourines...............13
   castanets.............................53
   concertinas........................47
   cymbals 65
   drum of the plain.............. 4
   Flutes...................................... 6
   frozen tambourines.......70

guitar 66
lonely guitars 35
slippery gong 6
tambourine 6

olives
　green olive 42
　olive grove 9
　olive groves 24, 39
　olive moon 42
　olive tree 8
　olive trees 6
　through the olive grove
　　they came 4

river 20, 21, 24, 31, 41, 42, 43, 46

rivers
　Guadalquivir 31, 41, 42, 43
　hidden rivers 25
　the riverside 19, 21, 32

saints
　Annunciation of the Kings
　　... 35
　Gabriel 36, 37
　Oh Gabriel 36
　Oh my little Gabriel! 36
　Saint Christopher 6
　Saint Eulalia 62
　SAINT EULALIA 60
　Saint Gabriel 35, 36
　SAINT GABRIEL 34
　Saint George 46
　Saint Joseph 53, 55
　Saint Michael 28, 29
　SAINT MICHAEL 27
　SAINT RAPHAEL 31
　St. Jame's 19
　The Virgin 53
　Virgin Mary 56

sea, ocean
　far from the sea 54
　ocean of profanity 47
　ocean waves 24
　sea 6, 11, 12, 15
　sea of bitterness 12
　swallowed by the sea ... 23
　the bay 39
　the sea he dances 28
　waves 5

silver 6, 7, 8, 11, 14, 19, 20, 27, 34, 45
　jars of silver coins 55
　silver armor chiming 62
　silver oil lamps 66
　silver tray 56, 61

slate 7, 48, 50

Spanish cities
　Albacete 8
　Almería 18
　Cordoba 31, 32, 33
　CORDOBA 31
　GRANADA 27
　Jerez de la Frontera 52, 53
　Merida 61
　MERIDA 60
　Seville 38
　SEVILLE 34, 38

stars ... 7, 11, 36, 37, 41, 56, 60
　Capricorn 39
　To the North there is one
　　star 67

sun 18

water 5, 13, 14, 24, 27, 32, 33, 38, 41, 53, 60, 64, 65, 66, 67
　a little water staircase .. 61
　Frenzied water 27
　snow-water 8
　the well 14

waves 31, 33

weapons
- a dozen spears 19
- arrows 74
- dagger blows 41
- dreams of handguns 51
- dusty daggers 39
- hazy broadsword 50
- heated rapier 6
- iron arrows 52
- Knives 61
- my blade 12
- my gun and holster 20
- riflemen 5
- rifles 55
- roses of black powder .. 56
- shiny knives 8
- thicket of knives 73
- wind .. 3, 4, 6, 9, 12, 14, 32, 36, 52, 64
- Now watching, watching is the air 4
- the biting wind 7
- the brutish wind 6

gyp·sy
/ˈjipsē/
noun

1. A member of a traveling people with dark skin and hair who speak Romany and traditionally live by seasonal work, itinerant trade, and fortune-telling. Gypsies are now found mostly in Europe, parts of North Africa, and North America, but are believed to have originated in South Asia.

2. A nomadic or free-spirited person.

Synonyms: Romany, Rom, traveler, nomad, rover, roamer, wanderer

www.ingramcontent.com/pod-product-compliance
Lightning Source LLC
Chambersburg PA
CBHW072023060426
42449CB00034B/1901